curries

igloo

igloo

Published by Igloo Books Ltd
Cottage Farm
Sywell
NN6 0BJ
www.igloo-books.com

10 9 8 7 6 5 4 3 2

ISBN: 978 1 84817 635 5

Project Managed by R&R Publications Marketing Pty Ltd

Food Photography: R&R Photostudio (www.rrphotostudio.com.au)
Recipe Development: R&R Test Kitchen

Front cover photograph © Stockfood/Jo Kirchherr

Printed and manufactured in India

contents

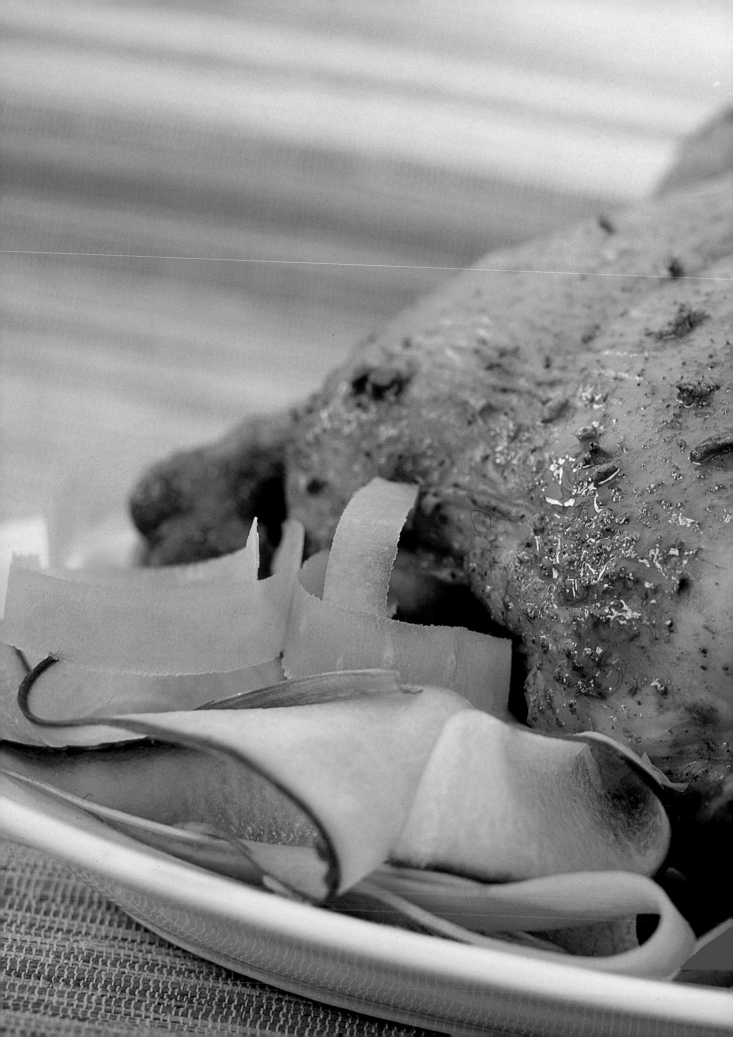

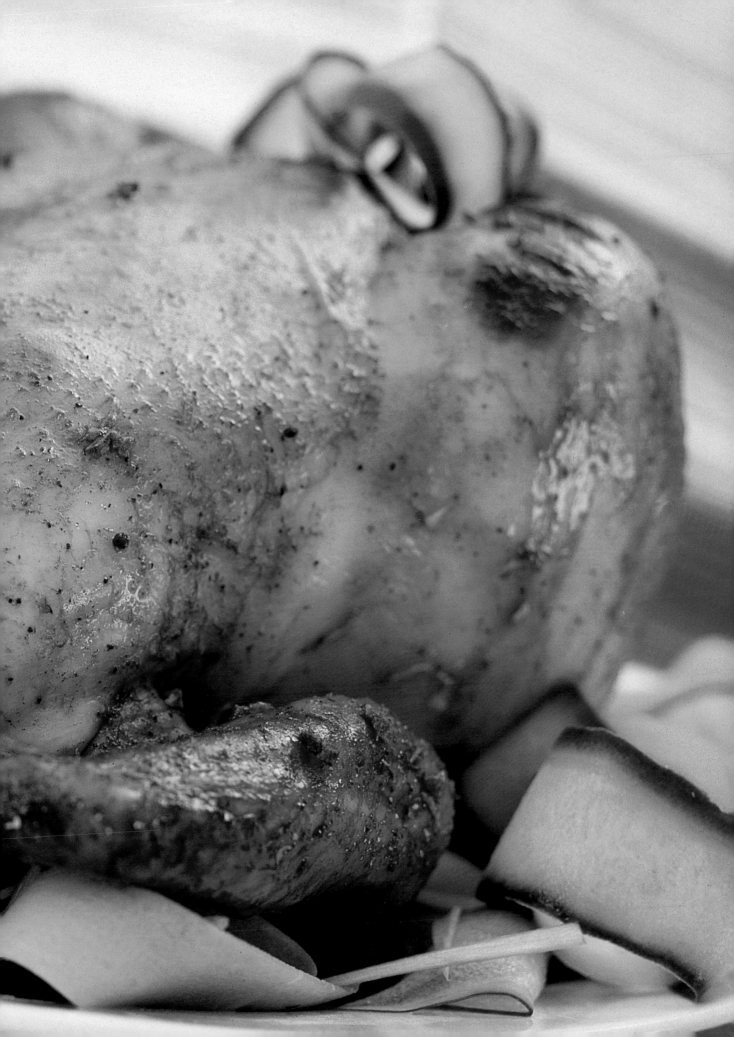

light and spicy

Spicy Chargrilled Vegetable Ciabatta

(see photograph on page 6)

1 large ciabatta

oil spray

about 4 cups mixed chargrilled
  vegetables such as peppers,
  aubergines and courgettes

½ cup mayonnaise

½ cup unsweetened natural yoghurt

1 teaspoon tandoori curry powder

2 tablespoons chopped fresh chives

1 tablespoon lemon juice

1   Cut ciabatta in half lengthwise. Spray with oil and grill until lightly golden. Remove from oven and arrange grilled vegetables over one half of the bread.

2   Mix mayonnaise, yoghurt, tandoori curry powder, chives and lemon juice together. Drizzle over vegetables. Top with remaining bread half. Cut into 2cm slices to serve.

Serves 4–6

Note: Buy chargrilled vegetables from the supermarket deli or make your own by brushing prepared vegetables with oil and grilling until golden and cooked.

Spicy Mexican Scrambled Eggs

(see photograph opposite)

4 flour tortillas

1 small onion

1 tablespoon butter

6 eggs

½ teaspoon chilli powder

½ teaspoon paprika

¼ cup milk

180g jar chunky salsa

2 tomatoes, to garnish

1 avocado, to garnish

1   Grill tortillas on both sides until lightly golden and keep warm. Peel onion and chop finely.

2   Melt butter in a frying pan and sauté onion for 5 minutes until clear. Lightly beat eggs, chilli powder, paprika and milk together. Pour into frying pan with onion and cook over a medium heat until egg begins to set. Drag a wooden spatula through egg mixture to allow uncooked egg to run through to the base of the pan. Spread salsa over tortillas to within 2cm of the edge. Pile scrambled eggs on top. Slice tomatoes. Peel, de-stone and slice avocado. Garnish eggs with tomato and avocado slices.

Serves 4

Note: Scrambled eggs should have large clots of egg rather than small grainy pieces. Dragging a wooden spatula through the egg mixture will give large clots. Don't stir your scrambled eggs as this will break up the clots and is more likely to cause them to go watery.

Spicy Lentil Soup

1 cup brown lentils

2 onions

2 cloves garlic

1 tablespoon oil

½ teaspoon chilli powder

1½ teaspoons hot curry powder

8 cups vegetable stock

2 tablespoons tomato paste

2 sticks celery

salt

freshly ground black pepper

1 Wash lentils and cover with cold water to soak while preparing rest of ingredients. Peel onions and chop finely. Crush, peel and chop garlic.

2 Heat oil in a large saucepan and sauté onion and garlic for 5 minutes. Add chilli powder and curry powder and cook for 30 seconds or until spices smell fragrant. Add stock and tomato paste to saucepan. Drain lentils and add to saucepan. Bring to the boil. Cover and simmer for 45 minutes or until lentils are tender.

3 Wash and slice celery finely. Stir through soup. Season with salt and pepper. Serve with crispy French bread.

Serves 4

Fish Laksa

CURRY PASTE

1 onion

2 cloves garlic

1 tablespoon Thai fish sauce (nam pla)

2 tablespoons roughly chopped fresh
  or preserved lemongrass

1 teaspoon shrimp paste

2cm peeled root ginger

2 whole chillies

1 teaspoon ground cumin

1 teaspoon ground coriander

LAKSA

2 tablespoons oil

2 cups fish stock

400ml can coconut milk

2 skinned and boned white-fleshed fish
  fillets

1 bundle egg noodles

2 tablespoons chopped fresh coriander

bean sprouts, to garnish

coriander leaves, to garnish

CURRY PASTE

1 Peel onion and chop roughly. Crush and peel garlic. Place onion, garlic and
   remaining curry paste ingredients in the bowl of a food processor or blender
   and process until finely chopped and combined.

LAKSA

1 Heat oil in a saucepan or clay pot and fry curry paste over a low heat for
   2–3 minutes or until spices smell fragrant. Add stock and coconut milk and
   bring to the boil. Cut fish into 2cm cubes. Add to laksa with noodles. Simmer
   for 3–4 minutes or until noodles and fish are cooked. Mix in fresh coriander
   and garnish with bean sprouts and coriander leaves if desired.

Serves 2

*Note: If you are short of time use a pot of ready-made laksa concentrate
instead of making this curry paste. Alternatively, use 1–2 tablespoons of
prepared red curry paste instead.*

Chorizo-Charged Curried Celeriac and Potato Soup

(see photograph opposite)

1 small celeriac bulb

4 medium potatoes

1 onion

2 tablespoons oil

1 tablespoon korma curry powder

5 cups vegetable stock

1 sliced chorizo sausage, to garnish

chives, to garnish

1 Peel celeriac and potatoes and cut into even-sized pieces. Peel onion and chop finely.

2 Heat oil in a saucepan and sauté onion and curry powder for 1 minute or until spices smell fragrant. Add stock and bring to the boil. Add celeriac and potato. Cover and simmer for 15–20 minutes or until vegetables are tender.

3 Mash with a potato masher or puree in a food processor or blender depending on the soup consistency you prefer.

4 Serve hot, garnished with chorizo slices and chives.

Serves 5

Note: Parsnip can be substituted for celeriac if desired.

Clay pots are available from Asian provision stores. They can be used on top of the stove as cooking pots and also double as serving vessels.

Celeriac is a vegetable that is part of the parsley family. It is a corm and other relatives include celery, parsnip and carrots. It is in season in autumn through the winter and sometimes into the spring. It has a fairly ugly appearance with a motley-brown, warty skin. If not cooked soon after peeling, celeriac will go brown. To stop this happening, pop it into a bowl of water with some lemon squeezed in. Celeriac can be mashed, pureed, boiled or chipped. It tastes like a cross between celery and parsnip.

Chicken Tortillas

2 cloves garlic, crushed

1 teaspoon ground cumin

½ teaspoon chilli powder

⅓ cup lime juice

1 tablespoon tequila

4 boneless chicken breast fillets

12 corn tortillas

1 red onion, sliced

½ bunch fresh coriander

Guacamole

roasted chilli salsa

½ cup sour cream (optional)

1 Place garlic, cumin, chilli powder, lime juice and tequila in a bowl and mix to combine. Add chicken, turn to coat, then cover and marinate for 30 minutes.

2 Drain chicken and cook on a preheated hot barbecue or char-grill in a frying pan for 3–4 minutes each side or until golden and cooked through. Cut chicken into slices.

3 Warm tortillas in a dry frying pan over a medium heat for 20–30 seconds each side or until heated through.

4 To serve, top each tortilla with chicken, onion and coriander leaves, fold or roll and accompany with bowls of Guacamole, salsa and sour cream, if using.

Makes 12

Quick Little Vegetable Samosas

4 sheets unsweetened shortcrust pastry

410g can potatoes

1 small onion

3 tablespoons peanut oil

1 teaspoon vindaloo curry powder

¼ cup frozen peas

¼ cup chopped fresh parsley

1 tablespoon lemon juice

1 Roll pastry out a little thinner. Cut five 10cm-diameter circles from each sheet of pastry. Cut circles in half.

2 Drain potatoes and chop finely. Peel onion and chop finely. Heat one tablespoon of oil in a frying pan and sauté onion for 5 minutes or until clear.

3 Add curry powder and cook for 30 seconds or until curry smells fragrant.

4 Mix potato, peas, onion mixture, parsley and lemon juice together.

5 Place a teaspoon of potato mixture on each semicircle. Wet pastry edges and fold dough over to form a cone shape. Cover with a damp tea towel while preparing remaining samosas.

6 Place on an oven tray and brush with half the remaining oil. Bake at 200°C for 15 minutes, turning after 10 minutes and brushing the other side with remaining oil.

Makes 40

Curried Pumpkin Soup

1 tablespoon polyunsaturated oil

1 large onion, chopped

½ teaspoon ground coriander

½ teaspoon ground cumin

½ teaspoon chilli powder

1 kg pumpkin, peeled and seeds removed

4 cups chicken stock

freshly ground black pepper

1 Heat oil in a large saucepan. Cook onion, coriander, cumin and chilli powder until onion softens.

2 Cut pumpkin into cubes and add to saucepan with stock. Cook pumpkin for 20 minutes or until tender, then cool slightly.

3 Transfer soup in batches to a food processor or blender and process until smooth. Return soup to a rinsed saucepan and heat. Season to taste with pepper.

Serves 4

Rice Cakes with Lime Crab

2 cups jasmine rice, cooked

30g fresh coriander leaves, chopped

crushed black peppercorns

vegetable oil for deep-frying

LIME CRAB TOPPING

185g canned crab meat, well-drained

2 fresh red chillies, seeded and chopped

2 small fresh green chillies, finely sliced

¼ cup coconut cream

2 tablespoons thick natural yogurt

3 teaspoons lime juice

3 teaspoons Thai fish sauce (nam pla)

3 teaspoons finely grated lime zest

1 tablespoon crushed black peppercorns

1 Combine rice, coriander and black peppercorns to taste, then press into an oiled 18 x 28cm shallow cake tin and refrigerate until set. Cut rice mixture into 3 x 4cm rectangles.

2 Heat vegetable oil in a large saucepan until a cube of bread dropped in browns in 50 seconds and cook rice cakes, a few at a time, for 3 minutes or until golden. Drain on absorbent kitchen paper.

3 To make topping, place crab meat, red and green chillies, coconut cream, yogurt, lime juice and fish sauce in a food processor and process until smooth. Stir in lime zest and black peppercorns. Serve with warm rice cakes.

Makes 24

Hot and Sour Seafood Soup

4 red or golden shallots, sliced

2 fresh green chillies, chopped

6 kaffir lime leaves

4 slices fresh ginger

8 cups fish, chicken or vegetable stock

250g boneless firm fish fillets, cut into chunks

12 medium uncooked prawns, shelled and deveined

12 mussels, scrubbed and beards removed

125g oyster or straw mushrooms

3 tablespoons lime juice

2 tablespoons Thai fish sauce (nam pla)

fresh coriander leaves

lime wedges

1 Place shallots, chillies, lime leaves, ginger and stock in a saucepan and bring to the boil over a high heat. Reduce heat and simmer for 3 minutes.

2 Add fish, prawns, mussels and mushrooms and cook for 3-5 minutes or until fish and seafood are cooked, discard any mussels that do not open after 5 minutes cooking. Stir in lime juice and fish sauce. To serve, ladle soup into bowls, scatter with coriander leaves and accompany with lime wedges.

Serves 6

Aztec Flower Soup

2 teaspoons vegetable oil

1 onion, finely chopped

1 clove garlic, crushed

2 tablespoons white rice

2 teaspoons chopped fresh marjoram

2 teaspoons chopped fresh thyme

8 cups chicken stock

12 courgette flowers

440g cooked or canned chickpeas, rinsed and drained

250g chopped cooked chicken

1 avocado, sliced

2 jalapeño chillies, sliced

1 tablespoon fresh coriander leaves

¼ onion, chopped

1 Heat oil in a saucepan over a medium heat, add onion and garlic and cook, stirring, for 3 minutes or until onion is soft. Add rice, marjoram, thyme and stock, bring to a simmering point and simmer for 15 minutes.

2 Remove the stamens and pistils from the zucchini (courgette) flowers by pinching with your fingers. Check that there are no insects hidden in the petals and wash flowers by dipping into water briefly. Trim stalks and set aside.

3 Add chickpeas, chicken and courgette flowers to soup and cook for 3 minutes or until flowers are tender.

4 To serve, ladle soup into bowls and top with avocado, chillies, coriander and onion.

Serves 6

Shellfish with Lemongrass

5 red or golden shallots, chopped

4 stalks fresh lemongrass, bruised and cut into 25mm pieces, or 2 teaspoons dried lemongrass, soaked in hot water until soft

3 cloves garlic, chopped

5cm piece fresh ginger, shredded

3 fresh red chillies, seeded and chopped

8 kaffir lime leaves, torn into pieces

750g mussels, scrubbed and beards removed

¼ cup water

12 scallops on shells, cleaned

1 tablespoon lime juice

1 tablespoon Thai fish sauce (nam pla)

3 tablespoons fresh basil leaves

1 Place shallots, lemongrass, garlic, ginger, chillies and lime leaves in a small bowl and mix to combine.

2 Place mussels in a wok and sprinkle over half the shallot mixture. Pour in water, cover and cook over a high heat for 5 minutes.

3 Add scallops, remaining shallot mixture, lime juice, fish sauce and basil and toss to combine. Cover and cook for 4–5 minutes or until mussels and scallops are cooked. Discard any mussels that do not open after 5 minutes.

Serves 4

Note: Serve this dish at the table straight from the wok and don't forget to give each diner some of the delicious cooking juices.

Cellophane Noodle Salad

155g cellophane noodles

2 teaspoons sesame oil

2 cloves garlic, crushed

1 tablespoon finely grated fresh ginger

500g pork mince

15g mint leaves

15g coriander leaves

8 lettuce leaves

5 red or golden shallots, chopped

1 fresh red chilli, sliced

2 tablespoons lemon juice

1 tablespoon light soy sauce

1 Place noodles in a bowl and pour over boiling water to cover. Stand for 10 minutes, then drain well.

2 Heat oil in a frying pan over a high heat, add garlic and ginger and stir-fry for 1 minute. Add pork and stir-fry for 5 minutes or until pork is browned and cooked through.

3 Arrange mint, coriander, lettuce, shallots, chilli and noodles on a serving platter. Top with pork mixture, then drizzle with lemon juice and soy sauce.

Serves 4

Note: Cellophane noodles also known as glass noodles and bean thread noodles or vermicelli are made from mung bean flour and are either very thin vermicelli-style noodles or flatter fettuccine-style noodles. In the dried state they are very tough and difficult to break. For ease of use it is best to buy a brand which packages them in bundles.

meat

Slow-Cooked Beef Curry

(see photograph on page 22)

800g blade, topside or chuck steak

3 onions

2 cloves garlic

2 tablespoons oil

1 tablespoon prepared minced ginger

3 tablespoons Kashmiri curry powder

1 teaspoon cracked black pepper

½ cup soy sauce

2 cups beef stock

290g can tomato puree

unsweetened natural yoghurt, to
 garnish

cucumber slices, to garnish

1 Cut fat from meat and discard. Cut meat into 2cm-wide strips about 6cm long. Peel onions and slice thinly. Crush, peel and chop garlic.

2 Heat oil in a saucepan large enough to cook the curry and sauté onions and garlic until brown. Add ginger and curry powder and cook for 1 minute. Mix in pepper, soy sauce, stock and tomato puree. Add meat. Cover and simmer for 1½ hours or until meat is tender.

3 Serve garnished with yoghurt and cucumber slices.

Serves 6

Hot-to-Trot Tabasco Steaks with Roasted Tomato Salsa

(see photograph opposite)

4 pieces thick-cut fillet steak

3 teaspoons Tabasco sauce

3 tablespoons cracked black pepper

ROASTED TOMATO SALSA

6 tomatoes

1 small onion

4 cloves garlic

3 tablespoons oil

½ teaspoon chilli powder

¼ cup chopped fresh parsley

1 teaspoon sugar

½ teaspoon salt

3 tablespoons red wine vinegar

1 Trim fat from steaks if necessary. Using the back of a teaspoon, rub Tabasco sauce over both sides of steaks.

2 Press on black pepper and grill or barbecue steaks until cooked as desired. Serve with roasted tomato salsa.

ROASTED TOMATO SALSA

1 Slash tops of tomatoes and place in an ovenproof dish. Bake at 190°C for 20 minutes.

2 Peel and finely chop onion. Crush, peel and chop garlic. Heat oil in a frying pan and cook onion and garlic until lightly golden. Add chilli powder and cook for 1 minute or until it smells fragrant. Roughly chop tomatoes, removing core. Mix tomatoes, parsley, sugar, salt and vinegar into onion mixture. Serve hot.

Serves 4

Curried Mango Sausages

8 sausages

1 cup rice

3 sticks celery

1 apple

1 tablespoon Madras curry powder

1 teaspoon mustard seeds

2 cups chicken stock

1 cup mango puree

1 Place sausages and rice in an ovenproof dish. Trim celery and slice. Peel, core and slice apple. Arrange celery and apple over sausages. Mix curry powder, mustard seeds and stock together. Add mango puree and pour over sausages.

2 Cover and bake at 180°C for 1 hour or until sausages are cooked. Serve with your choice of vegetables or fresh green salad.

Serves 4

Curry and Rice

500g lean mince steak

2 onions

1 tablespoon mild curry powder

¼ cup tomato relish, chutney or pickle

½ cup sultanas

2 cups beef stock

1 tablespoon plain flour

¼ cup water

2 tablespoons toasted coconut, to garnish

banana slices, to garnish

1 Place meat in a large saucepan. Cook over a medium heat, breaking up with a fork, until browned.

2 Peel onions and chop finely. Add to meat and cook for 5 minutes. Mix in curry powder, relish, sultanas and stock. Cook for 20 minutes.

3 Mix flour to a smooth paste with water and stir into meat mixture. Cook, stirring, until mixture boils and thickens. Serve garnished with toasted coconut and banana slices over steamed rice.

Serves 6

Vietnamese Pork

(see photograph opposite)

500g lean pork mince

1 clove garlic

2 spring onions

1 teaspoon sugar

1 tablespoon Thai fish sauce (nam pla)

200g dried egg noodles

small spinach leaves

basil leaves

HANOI SAUCE

1 clove garlic

1 tablespoon Thai fish sauce (nam pla)

¼ cup lime juice

2 dried chillies

½ teaspoon sugar

1 Place pork in a bowl. Crush, peel and finely chop garlic. Trim green onions and chop finely. Add garlic, green onions, sugar and fish sauce to pork. Mix well to combine.

2 Form tablespoonfuls of mixture into balls and flatten between your hands to form small patties.

3 Cook under a hot grill, on the barbecue or in a frying pan until lightly golden and cooked.

4 Cook noodles in boiling water to packet directions. Put cooked noodles in four serving bowls. Top with spinach leaves, pork patties and basil leaves.

5 Spoon Hanoi sauce over and serve.

HANOI SAUCE

1 Crush, peel and finely chop garlic. Mix garlic, fish sauce, lime juice, chillies and sugar together. Stand for an hour to let flavours develop.

Serves 4

Notes: If time is short, use ½ teaspoon of prepared minced chilli to replace dried chillies for a quick flavour fix.

Chillies are part of the Capsicum family and come in various sizes, shapes and flavours. Birdseye chillies are the very hot variety. They can be used fresh, dried or ground. If using fresh chillies, wear rubber gloves if possible when seeding and chopping the chillies. There is many a tale told of eye rubbing and other more gruesome experiences from hands used to prepare chillies. It can take many washings before the effect of the chillies is removed from your hands.

Cashew and Chilli Beef Curry

25mm piece fresh galangal or ginger, chopped or 5 slices bottled galangal, chopped

1 stalk fresh lemongrass, finely sliced, or ½ teaspoon dried lemongrass, soaked in hot water until soft

3 kaffir lime leaves, finely shredded

2 small fresh red chillies, seeded and chopped

2 teaspoons shrimp paste

2 tablespoons Thai fish sauce (nam pla)

1 tablespoon lime juice

2 tablespoons peanut oil

4 red or golden shallots, sliced

2 cloves garlic, chopped

3 small fresh red chillies, sliced

500g rump or blade steak, cut into 25mm cubes

2 cups beef stock

250g okra, trimmed

60g cashews, roughly chopped

1 tablespoon palm or brown sugar

2 tablespoons light soy sauce

1 Place galangal or ginger, lemongrass, lime leaves, chopped chillies, shrimp paste, fish sauce and lime juice in a food processor and process to make a thick paste, adding a little water if necessary.

2 Heat 1 tablespoon oil in a wok or large saucepan over a medium heat, add shallots, garlic, sliced red chillies and spice paste and cook, stirring, for 2–3 minutes or until fragrant. Remove and set aside.

3 Heat remaining oil in wok over a high heat and stir-fry beef, in batches, until brown. Return spice paste to pan, stir in stock and okra and bring to the boil. Reduce heat and simmer, stirring occasionally, for 15 minutes.

4 Stir in cashews, sugar and soy sauce and simmer for 10 minutes longer or until beef is tender.

Serves 4

Beef Tostada Cups

vegetable oil for deep-frying

8 corn tortillas

BEEF FILLING

2 teaspoons mild chilli powder

1 teaspoon ground cumin

¼ cup lime juice

500g rump steak, trimmed of visible fat

2 red onions, sliced

½ bunch coriander

1 Heat oil in a saucepan until a cube of bread dropped in browns in 50 seconds. Deep-fry tortillas, one at a time pressed between two metal ladles, for 1 minute or until crisp and golden. Drain on absorbent kitchen paper.

2 To make filling, place chilli powder, cumin and lime juice in a glass or ceramic dish and mix to combine. Add steak, turn to coat and marinate for 5 minutes. Drain steak and cook on a preheated barbecue or under a grill for 2-3 minutes each side or until cooked to your liking. Rest steak for 2 minutes, then cut into strips and place in a bowl. Add onions and coriander leaves and toss to combine.

3 To serve, divide filling between tostada cups and serve immediately.

Makes 8

Note: Serve these tasty snacks with salsas of your choice and lime wedges.

Spicy Beef Burger

500g lean beef mince

½ teaspoon chilli powder

¼ cup chopped fresh coriander

¼ cup chopped fresh basil

1 tablespoon chopped fresh mint

1 tablespoon prepared minced ginger

1 tablespoon Kashmiri curry powder

4 toasted naan bread

salad leaves

tomato or lime relish

1 Mix mince, chilli powder, coriander, basil, mint, ginger and curry powder together until combined. Divide mixture into four and form into patties by rolling into balls then flattening.

2 Cook in a frying pan or grill for 3–4 minutes each side or until cooked. Cut naan bread in half crosswise. Cover one half with salad leaves. Top with hamburger patty, relish and second piece of naan bread.

Makes 4

Note: Heat naan bread in the microwave on high power for 45–60 seconds or in the oven at 150°C for 3–5 minutes.

Tandoori Meatball Curry

1 small onion

500g lean lamb mince

1 tablespoon minced ginger

1 teaspoon garam masala

TANDOORI SAUCE

1 small onion

1 tablespoon oil

1 tablespoon tandoori curry powder

1 cup unsweetened natural yoghurt

1 tablespoon tomato pureé

1 tablespoon chopped fresh mint

1 Peel and finely chop onion. Mix mince, onion, ginger and garam masala together until combined.

2 Roll tablespoonfuls into balls. Bake at 180°C for 20 minutes or until cooked. Serve over steamed rice with tandoori sauce drizzled over.

TANDOORI SAUCE

1 Peel onion and chop finely. Heat oil in a frying pan and sauté onion for 5 minutes. Add curry powder and cook for 1 minute or until curry smells fragrant. Mix in yoghurt, tomato pureé and mint. Heat but do not boil.

2 Serve over meatballs.

Serves 4

Lamb Rendang

(see photograph opposite, top)

750g lamb steaks

¼ cup toasted desiccated coconut

1 onion

3 cloves garlic

3 tablespoons sliced fresh or prepared
lemongrass

2 teaspoons prepared minced chilli

1 tablespoon prepared minced ginger

1 teaspoon ground cumin

1 teaspoon ground turmeric

½ teaspoon salt

400g can coconut milk

½ cup water

1 cinnamon stick

1 Cut lamb into cubes. Place in a saucepan with toasted coconut. Peel onion and chop finely. Crush, peel and chop garlic. Add to pan with lemongrass, chilli, ginger, cumin, turmeric, salt, coconut milk, water and cinnamon stick.

2 Simmer, uncovered, for 1–1½ hours or until the meat is tender and the liquid almost all evaporated. Remove cinnamon stick and serve over steamed rice. Garnish with thin strips of green onion.

Serves 4

Note: Mixing your own spices to make curry flavours is always an adventure, so experiment and have fun. Use beef, pork or chicken instead of lamb for this dish if desired. Toast coconut over a low heat in a frying pan until starting to colour. Remove from heat as it will continue to cook.

Spicy Rubbed Lamb

(see photograph opposite, bottom)

1kg lamb rump

3 cloves garlic

1 cup chopped fresh parsley

1 teaspoon ground cumin

1 teaspoon ground cardamom

1 teaspoon cracked black pepper

½ teaspoon chilli powder

¼ cup olive oil

1 Remove silverskin from lamb. Crush, peel and finely chop garlic. Mix garlic, parsley, spices and oil together. Rub lamb all over with parsley mixture.

2 Stand for 1 hour before barbecuing or grilling until cooked as desired, or cooking at 230°C for 20 minutes. Let stand for 10 minutes. Serve on platter on a bed of salad leaves.

Serves 8–10

Note: Allow meat to stand after cooking and remember the meat will continue to cook on standing so remove from the grill, barbecue or oven slightly underdone.

Sweet Lamb Chop Curry

6 forequarter lamb chops

1 tablespoon olive oil

1 large onion, finely chopped

1 clove garlic, crushed

1½ tablespoons Madras-style curry powder

½ teaspoon ground ginger

2 cups water

salt and pepper

¾ cup mixed dried fruit

1 teaspoon brown sugar

½ cinnamon stick

½ cup plain yoghurt (optional)

1 Trim any excess fat from the chops. Wipe over with kitchen paper. Heat the oil in a large, heavy-based saucepan or lidded skillet. Add the onion and garlic and fry until golden over moderate heat. Remove the onion with a slotted spoon and set aside. Increase the heat and brown chops quickly on both sides. Do only 2–3 at a time. Remove to a plate and drain almost all fat from the pan.

2 Add the curry powder and ginger to the hot saucepan and stir over heat to roast until aroma rises. Stir in the water, lifting the pan juices as you stir. Season with salt and pepper.

3 Return the lamb and onion to the pan, cover and simmer for 1 hour. Add the dried fruit, sugar and cinnamon stick, and simmer for approximately 1 hour, until the lamb is very soft and tender. Add more water during cooking if necessary. Remove the chops to a hot serving platter. Stir the yoghurt into the sauce (if using) and pour the sauce over the chops. Serve with boiled rice.

Serves 4–6

Pork and Pumpkin Stir-fry

2 tablespoons Thai red curry paste

2 onions, cut into thin wedges, layers separated

2 teaspoons vegetable oil

500g lean pork strips

500g peeled pumpkin, cut into 2cm cubes

4 kaffir lime leaves, shredded

1 tablespoon palm or brown sugar

2 cups coconut milk

1 tablespoon Thai fish sauce (nam pla)

1 Place curry paste in wok and cook, stirring, over a high heat for 2 minutes or until fragrant. Add onions and cook for 2 minutes longer or until onions are soft. Remove from pan and set aside.

2 Heat oil in wok, add pork and stir-fry for 3 minutes or until brown. Remove pork from pan and set aside.

3 Add pumpkin, lime leaves, sugar, coconut milk and fish sauce to pan, bring to simmering and simmer for 2 minutes. Stir in curry paste mixture and simmer for 5 minutes longer. Return pork to pan and cook for 2 minutes or until heated.

Serves 4

Pork with Garlic and Pepper

2 teaspoons vegetable oil

4 cloves garlic, sliced

1 tablespoon crushed black peppercorns

500g lean pork strips

1 bunch/500g baby bok choy (Chinese greens), chopped

4 tablespoons fresh coriander leaves

2 tablespoons palm or brown sugar

2 tablespoons light soy sauce

2 tablespoons lime juice

1 Heat oil in a wok or frying pan over a medium heat, add garlic and black peppercorns and stir-fry for 1 minute. Add pork and stir-fry for 3 minutes or until brown.

2 Add bok choy, coriander, sugar, soy sauce and lime juice and stir-fry for 3-4 minutes or until pork and bok choy are tender.

Serves 4

Note: Bok choy is also known as Chinese chard, buck choy and pak choi. It varies in length from 10–30cm. For this recipe the smaller variety is used. It has a mild, cabbage-like flavour. Ordinary cabbage could be used for this recipe.

Red Beef Curry

1 cup coconut cream

3 tablespoons Thai red curry paste

500g rump or blade steak, cubed

160g pea aubergines or 1 large
  aubergine, diced

250g canned sliced bamboo shoots

6 kaffir lime leaves, crushed

1 tablespoon brown sugar

2 cups coconut milk

2 tablespoons Thai fish sauce (nam pla)

3 tablespoons fresh coriander leaves

2 fresh red chillies, chopped

1   Place coconut cream in a saucepan and bring to the boil over a high heat,
    then boil until oil separates from coconut cream and it reduces and thickens
    slightly. Stir in curry paste and boil for 2 minutes or until fragrant.

2   Add beef, aubergines, bamboo shoots, lime leaves, sugar, coconut milk and
    fish sauce, cover and simmer for 35–40 minutes or until beef is tender. Stir in
    coriander and chillies.

Serves 4

Spiced Shredded Beef

750g boneless beef chuck, blade or brisket, trimmed of visible fat

1 onion, halved

2 cloves garlic, peeled

1 clove

2 teaspoons cumin seeds

8 cups water

GREEN CHILLI AND TOMATO SAUCE

2 teaspoons vegetable oil

1 onion, chopped

2 hot green chillies, chopped

440g canned tomatoes, undrained and chopped

1 Place beef, onion, garlic, clove, cumin seeds and water in a saucepan over a medium heat, bring to simmering and simmer, skimming the top occasionally, for 1½ hours or until beef is very tender. Remove pan from heat and cool beef in liquid. Skim fat from surface as it cools. Remove beef from liquid and shred with a fork. Reserve cooking liquid for making sauce.

2 To make sauce, heat oil in a frying pan over a high heat, add onion and chillies and cook, stirring, for 3 minutes or until tender. Stir in tomatoes and 1 cup of the reserved cooking liquid, bring to simmering and simmer for 10 minutes or until mixture reduces and thickens.

3 Add shredded beef to sauce and simmer for 5 minutes or until heated through.

Serves 6

Pork and Marjoram Taquitos

12 corn tortillas, warmed

vegetable oil for shallow-frying

PORK AND MARJORAM FILLING

1 teaspoon vegetable oil

1 onion, chopped

2 fresh red chillies, chopped

2 cloves garlic, crushed

2 teaspoons ground cumin

500g pork mince

3 tablespoons chopped fresh marjoram

1 To make filling, heat oil in a frying pan over a high heat, add onion, chillies, garlic and cumin and cook, stirring, for 3 minutes or until onion and chillies are soft. Add pork and cook, stirring, for 3–4 minutes or until brown. Remove pan from heat, stir in marjoram and cool slightly.

2 Place 1 tablespoon of filling along the centre of each tortilla, then roll up and secure with wooden toothpicks or cocktail sticks.

3 Heat 1cm oil in a frying pan until a cube of bread dropped in browns in 50 seconds. Cook tortillas, a few at a time, for 1–2 minutes or until crisp. Drain on absorbent kitchen paper.

Makes 12

Santa Fe Grilled Beef

6 rib-eye steaks

1 avocado, sliced

lime wedges

2 spring onions, sliced

SPICE MIX

½ onion, very finely chopped

3 cloves garlic, crushed

1 tablespoon mild chilli powder

2 teaspoons grated lime zest

1 teaspoon ground cumin

2 tablespoons olive oil

1 tablespoon lime juice

1 To make spice mix, place onion, garlic, chilli powder, lime zest, cumin, oil and lime juice in a bowl and mix to combine.

2 Spread spice mix over both sides of each piece of steak and place between sheets of plastic food wrap. Pound with a meat mallet or rolling pin until steaks are 5mm thick.

3 Cook steaks on a preheated hot barbecue or in a frying pan for 30–60 seconds each side or until tender. Serve immediately with avocado slices, lime wedges and spring onions.

Serves 6

Note: For a complete meal add warm tortillas, Refried Beans and a lettuce salad.

Slow-Baked Chilli Lamb

1.5 kg leg lamb, trimmed of visible fat

CHILLI HERB PASTE

4 ancho chillies

3 cloves garlic, unpeeled

1 ripe tomato, peeled and chopped

1 tablespoon chopped fresh oregano

½ teaspoon ground cumin

½ teaspoon crushed black peppercorns

2 tablespoons apple cider vinegar

1 To make chilli paste, place chillies and garlic in a hot dry frying pan or comal over a high heat and cook until skins are blistered and charred. Place chillies in a bowl, pour over hot water to cover and soak for 30 minutes. Drain chillies and discard water.

2 Squeeze garlic from skins. Place chillies, garlic, tomato, oregano, cumin, peppercorns and vinegar in a food processor or blender and process to make a purée.

3 Place lamb in a glass or ceramic dish, spread with chilli paste, cover and marinate in the refrigerator for at least 3 hours or overnight.

4 Transfer lamb to a baking dish and roast at 150°C for 3 hours or until tender.

Serves 6

Note: Slice lamb and serve with warm tortillas, vegetables and a selection of salsas.

chicken

Kaffir Lime Curry

(see photograph on page 46)

4 single boneless, skinless chicken
    breasts

1 onion

2 cloves garlic

1 tablespoon oil

2 tablespoons Thai green curry paste

1 tablespoon prepared minced ginger

1 tablespoon Thai fish sauce (nam pla)

5 kaffir lime leaves

400g can coconut milk

8 small bok choy

¼ cup torn basil leaves

1   Cut chicken breasts into thirds. Peel onion and cut into slices. Crush, peel and
    chop garlic.

2   Heat oil in a saucepan and sauté onion and garlic for 5 minutes. Add
    curry paste, ginger and fish sauce. Cook for 1 minute or until spices smell
    fragrant. Bend lime leaves in one or three places so they remain whole.
    Add lime leaves, coconut milk and chicken to saucepan. Cover and cook for
    10 minutes.

3   Wash bok choy and cut in half lengthwise. Add to curry mixture. Cook for
    5 minutes. Mix in basil. Serve over steamed rice.

Serves 4

*Note: Kaffir lime leaves are available fresh from some greengrocers or dried
from Asian provision stores. Bending or folding the leaves cracks them to
release more of the flavour when cooking. Use regular lime or lemon leaves if
you cannot source these flavour powerhouses.*

Mustard Chicken

(see photograph opposite)

4 single boneless, skinless chicken
    breasts

1 bay leaf

1 onion

3 tablespoons oil

1 tablespoon mustard seeds

¼ cup capers

½ cup roughly chopped pitted green
    olives

2 tablespoons prepared wholegrain
    mustard

¼ cup lemon juice

freshly ground black pepper

1 tablespoon chopped fresh parsley,
    to garnish

1   Place chicken in a lidded frying pan. Cover with water. Add bay leaf and
    simmer for 10 minutes or until chicken is cooked. Peel onion and chop finely.

2   Heat oil in a frying pan. Add onion and cook for 5 minutes or until clear.
    Add mustard seeds and cook for 1 minute. Add capers, olives, mustard and
    lemon juice. Heat for 1 minute.

3   Serve over chicken with freshly ground black pepper and garnished with
    Italian parsley.

Serves 4

Spicy Roast Chicken with Cucumber Salad

1 medium chicken

6 cloves garlic

¼ cup honey

1 tablespoon cracked black pepper

½ teaspoon ground cloves

1 teaspoon ground ginger

CUCUMBER SALAD

2 spring onions

1 lebanese cucumber

1 carrot

1 teaspoon sesame oil

1 tablespoon white vinegar

½ teaspoon sugar

1 Remove giblets from chicken. Turn wings under and tie legs together. Crush, peel and chop garlic. Mix garlic, honey, pepper, cloves and ginger together. Brush over chicken.

2 Roast at 180°C for 1¼–1½ hours or until cooked. Serve sliced with cucumber salad and char siu sauce.

CUCUMBER SALAD

1 Trim spring onions and slice thinly lengthwise. Using a potato peeler, cut cucumber into lengths down the long side of the cucumber. Discard seedy core. Cut carrot into long lengths with the potato peeler. Mix spring onions, cucumber, carrot, sesame oil, vinegar and sugar together, tossing to coat.

Serves 4–6

Quick Chicken Curry

1 onion

2 cloves garlic

1 tablespoon oil

1 tablespoon Thai green curry paste

500g chicken tenderloins

400ml can low-fat coconut cream

1 teaspoon chicken stock powder

1 tomato

1 tablespoon chopped fresh coriander

1 Peel onion and chop finely. Crush, peel and chop garlic.

2 Heat oil in a saucepan and sauté onion and garlic for 5 minutes or until clear. Add curry paste and cook for 1 minute or until spices smell fragrant. Add tenderloins, coconut cream and stock powder. Bring to the boil and simmer for 7 minutes or until tenderloins are cooked. Cut tomato in half and remove core. Cut flesh into cubes. Mix in coriander. Serve chicken over cooked rice or noodles, topped with tomato mixture.

Serves 4

Note: This is what I make when I have limited time and don't have a jar of ready-made curry sauce to help me out. It's so simple I'm almost ashamed to call it a recipe.

Chicken Phanaeng Curry

(see photograph opposite, top)

2 cups coconut milk

3 tablespoons Thai red curry paste

500g chicken breast fillets, sliced

250g snake (yard-long) or green beans

3 tablespoons unsalted peanuts, roasted
  and finely chopped

2 teaspoons brown or palm sugar

1 tablespoon Thai fish sauce (nam pla)

½ cup coconut cream

2 tablespoons fresh basil leaves

2 tablespoons fresh coriander leaves

sliced fresh red chilli

1   Place coconut milk in a saucepan and bring to the boil over a high heat,
    then boil until oil separates from coconut milk and it reduces and thickens
    slightly. Stir in curry paste and boil for 2 minutes or until fragrant.

2   Add chicken, beans, peanuts, sugar and fish sauce and simmer for
    5–7 minutes or until chicken is tender. Stir in coconut cream, basil and
    coriander. Serve garnished with slices of chilli.

    Serves 4

Chicken with Lime and Coconut

(see photograph opposite, bottom)

1kg chicken thigh or breast fillets,
  cut into thick strips

1 tablespoon Thai red curry paste

1 tablespoon vegetable oil

3 tablespoons palm or brown sugar

4 kaffir lime leaves

2 teaspoons finely grated lime rind

1 cup coconut cream

1 tablespoon Thai fish sauce (nam pla)

2 tablespoons coconut vinegar

3 tablespoons shredded coconut

4 fresh red chillies, sliced

1   Place chicken and curry paste in a bowl and toss to coat. Heat oil in a wok
    or large saucepan over a high heat, add chicken and stir-fry for 4–5 minutes
    or until lightly browned and fragrant.

2   Add sugar, lime leaves, lime rind, coconut cream and fish sauce and cook,
    stirring, over a medium heat for 3–4 minutes or until the sugar dissolves and
    caramelises.

3   Stir in vinegar and coconut and simmer until chicken is tender. Serve with
    chillies in a dish on the side.

    Serves 4

Satay Chicken

14 satay sticks

¼ cup crunchy peanut butter

1 tablespoon soy sauce

1 tablespoon lemon juice

1 tablespoon dry sherry

1 tablespoon prepared minced ginger

1 teaspoon medium curry powder

1 tablespoon honey

3 single boneless, skinless chicken
  breasts

1 Soak satay sticks in water. Mix peanut butter, soy sauce, lemon juice, sherry, ginger, curry powder and honey together. Cut chicken into thin strips. Place chicken in a dish and pour peanut mixture over. Marinate for 1 hour at room temperature or refrigerate overnight.

2 Thread chicken on to soaked satay sticks. Cook chicken on the barbecue or under a hot grill, basting regularly with the peanut mixture. Cook until chicken juices run clear. Serve with satay sauce.

Serves 4

Tandoori Chicken Kebabs

14 satay sticks

4 single boneless, skinless chicken
  breasts

½ cup unsweetened natural yoghurt

2 tablespoons tandoori curry powder

2 tablespoons chopped fresh coriander

1   Soak satay sticks in water. Cut chicken breasts into strips about 2cm wide.
Mix yoghurt and curry powder together in a shallow dish. Use to coat
chicken.

2   Thread chicken onto soaked satay sticks. Grill or barbecue for 10 minutes
or until chicken is cooked and chicken juice run clear. Serve sprinkled with
coriander.

Serves 4

Chicken Tikka

(see photograph opposite)

8 boneless, skinless chicken thighs

3 cloves garlic

1 tablespoon prepared minced ginger

1 tablespoon chicken tikka curry powder

½ cup unsweetened natural yoghurt

2 tablespoons tomato sauce

2 tablespoons lime juice

CARDAMOM GLAZE

½ teaspoon ground cardamom

1 teaspoon cracked black pepper

1 tablespoon oil

1 tablespoon lime juice

1 Cut chicken into 1.5cm-thick strips. Crush, peel and finely chop garlic. Mix garlic, ginger, curry powder, yoghurt, tomato sauce and lime juice together in a bowl. Add chicken and marinate for 1 hour or longer if possible.

2 Thread chicken on metal or wooden skewers and grill or barbecue until golden and cooked, basting with marinade mixture during cooking. Serve brushed with cardamom glaze on a bed of sliced limes.

CARDAMOM GLAZE

1 Mix all ingredients together.

Serves 6

Chicken in Pumpkin Seed Sauce

(see photograph page 47)

4 boneless chicken breast fillets

½ onion

2 cloves garlic

2 stalks fresh coriander

4 cups water

PUMPKIN SEED SAUCE

2 x 440g canned tomatillos, drained

12 serrano chillies

½ bunch fresh coriander

¼ onion, chopped

1 clove garlic

1½ cups green pumpkin seeds (pepitas)

3 tablespoons unsalted peanuts

1 Place chicken, onion, garlic, coriander stalks and water in a saucepan over a low heat, bring to simmering and simmer for 15 minutes. Remove chicken from liquid. Strain cooking liquid and discard solids. Reserve liquid for sauce.

2 To make sauce, place tomatillos, chillies, coriander leaves, onion and garlic in a food processor or blender and process until smooth.

3 Heat a frying pan over a medium heat, add pumpkin seeds (pepitas) and cook, stirring, for 3–4 minutes or until seeds pop and are golden. Place pumpkin seeds (pepitas) and peanuts in a clean food processor or blender and process to make a paste. Return nut paste to frying pan and cook, stirring, for 3 minutes or until golden. Gradually stir in tomatillo mixture and 2 cups of the reserved cooking liquid, bring to simmering and simmer, stirring frequently, for 10 minutes. Add chicken to sauce and simmer for 5 minutes or until heated through.

Serves 4

Curried Chicken Rolls

2 teaspoons canola oil

1 medium onion, finely chopped

1 small clove garlic, crushed

2 teaspoons mild curry paste

1½ tablespoon lemon juice

500g minced chicken meat

3 tablespoons dried breadcrumbs

½ teaspoon salt

½ teaspoon pepper

2 tablespoons chopped fresh coriander

2 sheets frozen puff pastry

1 tablespoon milk for glazing

1 tablespoon sesame seeds

1 Heat the oil in a small pan, add the onion and garlic and fry until onion is soft. Stir in the curry paste and cook a little. Add the lemon juice and stir to mix. Set aside. Combine the minced chicken, breadcrumbs, salt, pepper and coriander and add the onion/curry mixture. Mix well.

2 Place a thawed sheet of puff pastry on a work surface and cut in half across the centre. Pile quarter of the meat mixture in a thick 1½ cm wide strip along the centre of the strip. Brush the exposed pastry at the back with water, lift the front strip of pastry over the filling and roll to rest onto the back strip. Press lightly to seal. Cut the roll into 4–5 equal portions. Repeat with the second half and then with the second sheet. Glaze with milk and sprinkle with sesame seeds. Place onto a flat baking tray.

3 Cook in a preheated hot oven (190°) for 10 minutes, reduce heat to 180°C and continue cooking for 15 minutes until golden brown. Serve hot as finger food.

Serves 16–20

Note: Can be made in advance and reheated in a moderate oven.

Australian-Style Chicken Curry

500g chicken thigh fillets

2 tablespoons oil

1 large onion, finely chopped

250g can Madras curry cooking sauce

2 tablespoons sultanas

2 bananas, sliced

1 green apple, peeled, cored and cut
  into large dice

steamed rice to serve

1 Cut the chicken thighs into 2–3 pieces. Heat half the oil in a large saucepan, add third of the chicken and quickly brown on both sides. Remove to a plate and brown the remaining chicken in 2 batches, adding the remaining oil as necessary. Remove the last batch of chicken.

2 Add the onion and cook a little then stir in the Madras curry cooking sauce. Add a little water to the can to rinse down the remaining sauce (about a quarter can) and pour into the saucepan. Bring to the boil, turn down the heat and return the chicken to the saucepan. Cover and simmer for 20 minutes. Add the sultanas, banana and apple and simmer for 15–20 minutes more. Serve immediately with steamed rice.

Serves 2–3

Thai Green Chicken Curry

1 tablespoon vegetable oil

2 onions, chopped

3 tablespoons Thai green curry paste

1 kg boneless chicken thigh or breast
  fillets, chopped

4 tablespoons fresh basil leaves

6 kaffir lime leaves, shredded

2½ cups coconut milk

2 tablespoons Thai fish sauce (nam pla)

extra fresh basil leaves

1 Heat oil in a saucepan over a high heat, add onions and cook for 3 minutes
   or until golden. Stir in curry paste and cook for 2 minutes or until fragrant.

2 Add chicken, basil, lime leaves, coconut milk and fish sauce and bring to the
   boil. Reduce heat and simmer for 12–15 minutes or until chicken is tender
   and sauce is thick. Serve garnished with extra basil.

Serves 6

Note: The curry pastes of Thailand are mixtures of freshly ground herbs and
spices and if you are able to make your own it is well worth the small effort
required.

Thai Chicken Cakes

3 slices toast bread

250g skinless, boneless chicken

4 sprigs fresh coriander

1 teaspoon prepared minced chilli

3 tablespoon lime or lemon juice

1 egg white

cornflour

oil spray

thin strips celery

thin strips green onion

sweet chilli sauce

1 Remove crusts from bread. Break bread into pieces. Place bread, chicken, coriander, chilli, lime or lemon juice and egg white in the bowl of a food processor and process until roughly chopped and combined.

2 Divide mixture into eight portions. Shape into rounds about 7cm in diameter, tossing in cornflour to prevent sticking.

3 Spray a frying pan with oil spray and cook cakes for 2–3 minutes each side or until lightly golden and chicken is cooked.

4 Serve stacked on plates, garnished with thin strips of celery and green onion soaked in very cold water to make them curl. Drizzle with sweet chilli sauce.

Serves 4

Nyonya Chicken Stir-Fry and Spinach

500g boneless, skinless chicken

1 stalk fresh or preserved lemongrass

3 green onions

2 tablespoons oil

1 tablespoon prepared minced ginger

1 half bunch of spinach

1 teaspoon chilli powder

¼ cup lime juice

1 teaspoon sugar

½ cup coconut milk

1 tablespoon soy sauce

1 Cut chicken into thin strips. Trim lemongrass, slit lengthwise and chop very finely. Trim green onions and cut into 5mm slices on the diagonal.

2 Heat oil in a wok and stir-fry chicken in small batches. Remove each batch from wok and set aside. Stir-fry lemongrass, green onions, ginger and spinach for 3 minutes. Add chilli powder and cook for 1 minute or until chilli smells fragrant. Add lime juice, sugar, coconut milk and soy sauce to wok. Return chicken to wok. Heat and serve.

Serves 4

Note: The Nyonya people are descendants of Chinese and Malay marriages several centuries ago. They combine Malay and Chinese cooking to give a unique Asian blend of flavours.

Chicken with Garlic and Pepper

4 cloves garlic

3 fresh coriander roots

1 teaspoon crushed black peppercorns

500g chicken breast fillets, chopped
  into 25mm cubes

vegetable oil for deep-frying

30g fresh basil leaves

30g fresh mint leaves

sweet chilli sauce

1 Place garlic, coriander roots and black peppercorns in a food processor
  and process to make a paste. Coat chicken with garlic paste and marinate
  for 1 hour.

2 Heat oil in a wok or frying pan over a high heat until a cube of bread
  dropped in browns in 50 seconds, then deep-fry chicken, a few pieces at
  a time, for 2 minutes or until golden and tender. Drain on absorbent kitchen
  paper.

3 Deep-fry basil and mint until crisp, then drain and place on a serving plate.
  Top with chicken and serve with chilli sauce.

Serves 4

*Note: Thai cooks use three types of basil in cooking – Asian sweet, holy
and lemon – each has a distinctive flavour and is used for specific types of
dishes. For this dish Asian sweet basil, known in Thailand as horapa, would
be used.*

seafood

Fish Cakes with Chilli Cucumber Sauce

(see photograph on page 64)

3 skinned and boned white-fleshed fish fillets

1 teaspoon Thai red curry paste

¼ cup chopped fresh coriander

½ teaspoon grated lime zest

2 tablespoons lime juice

½ teaspoon salt

1 teaspoon prepared minced ginger

2 eggs

¼ cup cornflour

2 tablespoons oil

CHILLI CUCUMBER SAUCE

¼ cup finely chopped cucumber

1 tablespoon finely chopped red capsicum

¼ teaspoon chilli powder

¼ cup rice vinegar

1 teaspoon brown sugar

1 tablespoon chopped fresh coriander

1 Cut fish into chunks and place in the bowl of a food processor with curry paste, coriander, lime zest and juice, salt, ginger, eggs and cornflour. Process until coarsely chopped and combined.

2 Heat oil in a frying pan. Measure quarter-cupfuls of mixture and flatten to about 1cm thick in the pan. Cook until lightly golden. Turn and cook other side. Serve hot with chilli cucumber sauce.

CHILLI CUCUMBER SAUCE

1 Mix cucumber, capsicum, chilli powder, vinegar, sugar and coriander together.

Serves 4

Vulcan Lane Mussels

(see photograph opposite)

1 onion

2 cloves garlic

1 stalk fresh or preserved lemongrass

1 tablespoon oil

1 teaspoon chilli powder

2 teaspoons vindaloo curry powder

400g can low-fat coconut milk

1½ cups fish stock

36 fresh mussels in the shell

¼ cup lemon juice

chopped fresh coriander, to garnish

1 Peel onion and chop finely. Crush, peel and finely chop garlic. Trim lemongrass and slice very thinly.

2 Heat oil in a large saucepan. Sauté onion and garlic for 5 minutes or until clear. Add lemongrass, chilli powder and curry powder and cook for 1 minute or until spices smell fragrant. Pour in coconut milk and stock and bring to the boil.

3 Clean and de-beard mussels and add to boiling liquid. Cook, covered, for 5–6 minutes or until mussels open. Discard any mussels that do not open. Spoon mussels into serving bowls. Mix lemon juice into liquid and pour over mussels. Garnish with chopped fresh coriander.

Serves 4

Penang Fish Curry

4 skinned and boned white-fleshed
  fish fillets

2 onions

3 cloves garlic

1 red pepper

2 teaspoons sesame oil

1 teaspoon ground cumin

1 tablespoon mild curry powder

1 teaspoon mustard seeds

400g can chopped tomatoes in juice

½ cup fish stock

2 tablespoons chopped fresh coriander

1   Cut fish into large cubes. Peel onions and chop finely. Crush, peel and chop
    garlic. Halve, deseed and chop pepper into cubes.

2   Heat oil in a saucepan and sauté onion and garlic for 5 minutes or until
    clear, not coloured. Add cumin, curry powder, mustard seeds and red
    pepper. Cook for 1 minute or until spices smell fragrant. Add crushed
    tomatoes and stock. Bring to the boil and simmer for 5 minutes.

3   Add fish and simmer for 4–5 minutes or until fish is just cooked. Mix in
    coriander and serve.

Serves 4

Hot Baked Fish

1 whole scaled and gutted salmon or
  white-fleshed fish about 1kg in weight

3 whole chillies

2 teaspoons paprika

1 teaspoon ground cumin

12 fresh chives

8 fresh basil leaves

½ cup fresh parsley sprigs

1 tablespoon fish sauce

3 tablespoons peanut oil

1 Cut slashes in fish at about 2cm intervals. Place in an ovenproof dish. Place chillies, paprika, cumin, chives, basil, parsley, fish sauce and oil in the bowl of a food processor or blender. Blend until finely chopped.

2 Press mixture into slashes in fish and over skin. Bake at 180°C for 20–25 minutes or until just cooked. Serve with fresh mixed salad.

Serves 4

Barbecued Squid Salad

1 tablespoon chilli oil

1 tablespoon finely grated lemon rind

2 teaspoons crushed black peppercorns

500g small squid (calamari) hoods, cleaned

30g fresh basil leaves

30g fresh mint leaves

30g fresh coriander leaves

LEMON AND CHILLI DRESSING

1 fresh green chilli, chopped

2 tablespoons brown sugar

3 tablespoons lemon juice

2 tablespoons light soy sauce

1 Place oil, lemon rind and peppercorns in a shallow dish and mix to combine. Add squid (calamari) and marinate for 30 minutes.

2 Line a serving platter with the basil, mint and coriander. Cover with plastic food wrap and refrigerate until ready to serve.

3 To make dressing, place chilli, sugar, lemon juice and soy sauce in a bowl and mix to combine.

4 Preheat a barbecue, char-grill pan or frying pan and cook the squid (calamari) for 30 seconds each side or until tender – take care not to overcook or the squid will become tough. Place the squid on top of herbs and drizzle with dressing.

Serves 4

Coconut Prawns and Scallops

1kg large uncooked prawns, shelled and deveined, tails left intact

3 egg whites, lightly beaten

90g shredded coconut

vegetable oil for deep-frying

1 tablespoon peanut oil

4 fresh red chillies, seeded and sliced

2 small fresh green chillies, seeded and sliced

2 cloves garlic, crushed

1 tablespoon shredded fresh ginger

3 kaffir lime leaves, finely shredded

375g scallops

125g mangetout (snow pea) leaves or sprouts

2 tablespoons palm or brown sugar

¼ cup lime juice

2 tablespoons Thai fish sauce (nam pla)

1 Dip prawns in egg whites, then roll in coconut to coat. Heat vegetable oil in a large saucepan until a cube of bread dropped in browns in 50 seconds and cook prawns, a few at a time, for 2–3 minutes or until golden and crisp. Drain on absorbent kitchen paper and keep warm.

2 Heat peanut oil in a wok over a high heat, add red and green chillies, garlic, ginger and lime leaves and stir-fry for 2–3 minutes or until fragrant.

3 Add scallops to wok and stir-fry for 3 minutes or until opaque. Add cooked prawns, mangetout leaves or sprouts, sugar, lime juice and fish sauce and stir-fry for 2 minutes or until heated.

Serves 6

Green Chilli and Prawn Curry

1 tablespoon vegetable oil

1.5 kg medium uncooked prawns, shelled and deveined, shells and heads reserved

2 stalks fresh lemongrass, bruised, or 1 teaspoon dried lemongrass, soaked in hot water until soft

2 long fresh green chillies, halved

4 cm piece fresh galangal or ginger, or 6 slices bottled galangal

3 cups water

2 teaspoons Thai green curry paste

1 cucumber, seeded and cut into thin strips

5 whole fresh green chillies (optional)

1 tablespoon palm or brown sugar

2 tablespoons Thai fish sauce (nam pla)

1 tablespoon coconut vinegar

2 teaspoons tamarind concentrate

1 Heat 2 teaspoons oil in a saucepan over a medium heat, add reserved prawn shells and heads and cook, stirring, for 3–4 minutes or until shells change colour. Add lemongrass, the halved green chillies, galangal or ginger and water and bring to the boil. Using a wooden spoon break up galangal or ginger, reduce heat and simmer for 10 minutes. Strain, discard solids and set stock aside.

2 Heat remaining oil in a wok or saucepan over a medium heat and stir-fry curry paste for 2–3 minutes or until fragrant.

3 Add prawns, cucumber, 5 whole green chillies (if using), sugar, reserved stock, fish sauce, vinegar and tamarind and cook, stirring, for 4–5 minutes or until prawns change colour and are cooked through.

Serves 4

Note: Fresh lemongrass is available from Asian food shops and some supermarkets and greengrocers. It is also available dried; if using dried lemongrass soak it in hot water for 20 minutes or until soft before using. Lemongrass is also available in bottles from supermarkets, use this in the same way as you would fresh lemongrass.

Stir-Fried Tamarind Prawns

2 tablespoons tamarind pulp

½ cup water

2 teaspoons vegetable oil

3 stalks fresh lemongrass, chopped, or
  2 teaspoons finely grated lemon rind

2 fresh red chillies, chopped

500g medium uncooked prawns,
  shelled and deveined, tails intact

2 green (unripe) mangoes, peeled
and thinly sliced

3 tablespoons chopped fresh coriander
  leaves

2 tablespoons brown sugar

2 tablespoons lime juice

1 Place tamarind pulp and water in a bowl and stand for 20 minutes. Strain, reserve liquid and set aside. Discard solids.

2 Heat oil in a wok or frying pan over a high heat, add lemongrass or rind and chillies and stir-fry for 1 minute. Add prawns and stir-fry for 2 minutes or until they change colour.

3 Add mangoes, coriander, sugar, lime juice and tamarind liquid and stir-fry for 5 minutes or until prawns are cooked.

Serves 4

Note: Tamarind is the large pod of the tamarind or Indian date tree. After picking, it is seeded and peeled, then pressed into a dark brown pulp. It is also available as a concentrate. Tamarind pulp or concentrate can be purchased from Indian food stores. In Oriental cooking it is used as a souring agent, if unavailable a mixture of lime or lemon juice and treacle can be used instead.

Fish with Green Mango Sauce

4 x 200g firm fish fillets or cutlets

4 pieces banana leaf, blanched

3 cloves garlic, sliced

1 tablespoon shredded fresh ginger

2 kaffir lime leaves, shredded

GREEN MANGO SAUCE

½ small green (unripe) mango,
flesh grated

3 red or golden shallots, chopped

2 fresh red chillies, sliced

1 tablespoon brown sugar

¼ cup water

1 tablespoon Thai fish sauce (nam pla)

1   Place a fish fillet or cutlet in the centre of each banana leaf. Top fish with a little each of the garlic, ginger and lime leaves, then fold over banana leaves to enclose. Place parcels over a charcoal barbecue or bake at 180°C in the oven for 15–20 minutes or until fish flakes when tested with a fork.

2   To make sauce, place mango, shallots, chillies, sugar, water and fish sauce in a saucepan and cook, stirring, over a low heat for 4–5 minutes or until sauce is heated through.

3   To serve, place parcels on serving plates, cut open to expose fish and serve with sauce.

Serves 4

Note: Banana leaves are used in South-East Asian and Pacific countries in much the same way as Westerners use aluminium foil. Foil can be used if banana leaves are unavailable, however the finished dish will not have the flavour that the banana leaf contributes and it may be slightly drier.

Deep-fried Chilli Fish

2 x 500g whole fish such as bream, snapper, whiting, sea perch, cod or haddock, cleaned

4 fresh red chillies, chopped

4 fresh coriander roots

3 cloves garlic, crushed

1 teaspoon crushed black

peppercorns

vegetable oil for deep-frying

RED CHILLI SAUCE

⅔ cup sugar

8 fresh red chillies, sliced

4 red or golden shallots, sliced

⅓ cup coconut vinegar

⅓ cup water

1 Make diagonal slashes along both sides of the fish.

2 Place chopped chillies, coriander roots, garlic and black peppercorns in a food processor and process to make a paste. Spread mixture over both sides of fish and marinate for 30 minutes.

3 To make sauce, place sugar, sliced chillies, shallots, vinegar and water in a saucepan and cook, stirring, over a low heat until sugar dissolves. Bring mixture to simmering and simmer, stirring occasionally, for 4 minutes or until sauce thickens.

4 Heat vegetable oil in a wok or deep-frying pan until a cube of bread dropped in browns in 50 seconds. Cook fish, one at a time, for 2 minutes each side or until crisp and flesh flakes when tested with a fork. Drain on absorbent kitchen paper. Serve with chilli sauce.

Serves 6

Prawn Empanadas

Vegetable oil for deep-frying

EMPANADA DOUGH

2¾ cups flour

60g soft butter

¾ cup warm water

CHILLI AND PRAWN FILLING

2 teaspoons vegetable oil

1 onion, chopped

1 tablespoon fresh oregano leaves

2 teaspoons fresh lemon thyme leaves

500g peeled uncooked prawns

2 green tomatoes, peeled and chopped

4 poblano chillies, roasted, seeded and peeled and chopped

1 To make dough, place flour and butter in a food processor and process until mixture resembles coarse breadcrumbs. With machine running, add enough of the warm water to form a smooth dough. Knead dough on a lightly floured surface for 3 minutes, then divide into 12 portions. Cover with a damp cloth and set aside.

2 To make filling, heat oil in a frying pan over medium heat, add onion, oregano and thyme and cook for 4 minutes or until onions are golden. Add prawns, tomatoes and chillies and simmer for 5 minutes or until mixture reduces and thickens. Cool.

3 Roll each portion of dough out to form an 18cm circle about 3mm thick. Place 3 tablespoons of filling on one half of each dough round, then fold over to enclose filling and pinch edges to seal.

4 Heat oil in a saucepan until a cube of bread dropped in browns in 50 seconds, then cook empanadas, a few at a time, for 2–3 minutes or until crisp and golden. Drain on absorbent kitchen paper and serve.

Makes 12

Fish with Lime and Garlic

750g whole fish such as sea perch, sea
  bass, coral trout or snapper, cleaned

2 stalks fresh lemongrass, chopped, or
  1 teaspoon dried lemongrass, soaked
  in hot water until soft

4 slices fresh ginger

1 fresh green chilli, halved

4 kaffir lime leaves, crushed

8 whole fresh coriander plants

LIME AND GARLIC SAUCE

2 fresh red chillies, seeded and
  chopped

2 green chillies, seeded and chopped

3 cloves garlic, chopped

1 tablespoon shredded fresh ginger

1 cup fish or chicken stock

4 tablespoons lime juice

1 tablespoon Thai fish sauce (nam pla)

1 Cut deep diagonal slits in both sides of the fish. Place lemongrass, ginger,
   the halved green chilli, lime leaves and coriander plants in cavity of fish.

2 Half fill a wok with hot water and bring to the boil. Place fish on a wire rack
   and place above water. Cover wok and steam for 10–15 minutes or until
   flesh flakes when tested with a fork.

3 To make sauce, place red and green chillies, garlic, ginger, stock, lime juice
   and fish sauce in a small saucepan, bring to simmering over a low heat and
   simmer for 4 minutes. To serve, place fish on a serving plate and spoon over
   sauce.

Serves 4

Prawn Tostaditas

vegetable oil

8 corn tortillas

½ avocado, chopped

2 tablespoons shredded fresh mint

PRAWN AND VEGETABLE TOPPING

1 cob sweetcorn

1 red pepper, quartered

1 yellow pepper, quartered

1 red onion, cut into wedges

375g medium uncooked prawns,
  shelled and deveined

4 mild fresh green chillies, cut into strips
  1 tablespoon lime juice

1 To make topping, place sweetcorn cob and red and yellow peppers on a preheated hot barbecue or char-grill and cook until lightly charred. Cut corn kernels from cob and set aside. Cut peppers into strips and set aside.

2 Heat 2 teaspoons of oil in a frying pan over a medium heat, add onion and cook for 4 minutes or until golden. Add prawns, chillies and lime juice and cook for 2 minutes or until prawns change colour. Add sweet corn kernels and red and yellow peppers, toss to combine and set aside.

3 Heat 25mm oil in a frying pan over a medium heat until a cube of bread dropped in browns in 50 seconds. Cook tortillas, one at time, for 45 seconds each side or until crisp. Drain on absorbent kitchen paper.

4 To serve, pile topping onto tortillas, then scatter with avocado and mint. Serve immediately.

Serves 4

Barbecue Chilli Prawns

1 kg medium uncooked prawns, in their shells

250g chopped pawpaw

2 tablespoons chopped fresh mint

lime wedges

sliced chillies

ORANGE MARINADE

2 tablespoons mild chilli powder

2 tablespoons chopped fresh oregano

2 cloves garlic, crushed

2 teaspoons grated orange zest

2 teaspoons grated lime zest

¼ cup orange juice

¼ cup lime juice

1 To make marinade, place chilli powder, oregano, garlic, orange and lime zest and orange and lime juices in a bowl and mix to combine. Add prawns, toss, cover and marinate in the refrigerator for 1 hour.

2 Drain prawns and cook on a preheated hot char-grill or barbecue plate (griddle) for 1 minute each side or until they change colour.

3 Place pawpaw and mint in bowl and toss to combine. To serve, pile prawns onto serving plates, top with pawpaw mixture and accompany with lime wedges and sliced chillies.

Serves 4

Fish Baked in Corn Husks

16–24 dried corn husks

4 firm white fish fillets

3 tablespoons fresh coriander leaves

1 avocado, sliced

pickled jalapeño chillies

corn or flour tortillas, warmed

CHILLI LIME PASTE

3 cloves garlic, chopped

2 mild fresh green chillies, chopped

2 tablespoons fresh oregano leaves

2 tablespoons mild chilli powder

2 teaspoons grated lime rind

1 teaspoon ground cumin

¼ cup lime juice

1 Place corn husks in a bowl, pour over warm water to cover and soak for 30 minutes.

2 To make chilli paste, place garlic, chillies, oregano, chilli powder, lime rind, cumin and lime juice in a food processor or blender and process until smooth.

3 Cut each fish fillet in half, then spread both sides with chilli paste.

4 Overlap 2–3 corn husks, place a piece of fish on top, then cover with more husks, fold to enclose fish and tie to secure. Place parcels on a baking tray and bake at 180°C for 10–12 minutes or until flesh flakes when tested with a fork.

5 To serve, open fish parcels, scatter with coriander and accompany with avocado, chillies and tortillas.

Serves 4

Note: Corn husks and banana leaves are used extensively in Mexico as wrappers for edible parcels. Corn husks are favoured in northern Mexico while banana leaves are more popular in southern and coastal areas.

Roasted Garlic Fish

1.5 kg whole fish such as bream, snapper, whiting, sea perch, cod or haddock, cleaned

1 lemon, sliced

2 fresh red chillies, halved

3 sprigs fresh marjoram

7 cloves garlic, unpeeled

2 tablespoons butter

⅓ cup coconut milk

1 Pat fish dry with absorbent kitchen paper. Place fish in a baking dish and fill cavity with lemon slices, chillies and marjoram sprigs.

2 Place garlic in a hot frying pan or comal and cook until skins are charred and garlic is soft. Squeeze garlic from skins into a bowl, add butter and mix to combine. Spread garlic butter over both sides of fish, cover with foil and bake at 150°C for 40 minutes or until flesh flakes when tested with a fork. Remove foil, place under a hot grill and cook for 3–4 minutes each side or until skin is crisp. To serve, drizzle with coconut milk.

Serves 4

Note: Serve fish with Mexican Red Rice or tortillas and a salad.

Seafood Tacos

8 flour tortillas, warmed

155g feta cheese crumbled

SEAFOOD FILLING

2 teaspoons vegetable oil

1 onion, chopped

2 tomatoes, chopped

375g white fish, cubed

250g shelled and deveined medium uncooked prawns

12 scallops

3 medium fresh green chillies, chopped

2 tablespoons chopped fresh oregano

1 teaspoon finely grated lemon rind

1 To make filling, heat oil in a frying pan over a high heat, add onion and cook for 4 minutes or until golden. Add tomatoes and cook for 5 minutes. Add fish, prawns, scallops, chillies, oregano and lemon zest and cook, tossing, for 3–4 minutes or until seafood is cooked.

2 To serve, spoon filling down the centre of each tortilla and scatter with feta cheese. Fold tortilla to enclose filling and serve immediately.

Serves 4

Note: These indulgent tacos are wonderful served with Garlic and Chilli Salsa.

Grilled Scallops with Salsa

30 scallops

chilli or lime oil

crisp tortilla chips

PINEAPPLE SALSA

125g chopped pineapple

¼ red pepper, finely chopped

2 medium green chillies, chopped

1 tablespoon fresh coriander leaves

1 tablespoon fresh mint leaves

1 tablespoon lime juice

1 To make salsa, place pineapple, red pepper, chillies, coriander, mint and lime juice in a bowl, toss to combine, then stand for 20 minutes.

2 Brush scallops with oil and cook on a preheated hot char-grill or barbecue plate (griddle) for 30 seconds each side or until they just change colour. Serve immediately with salsa and tortilla chips.

Serves 4

Note: To make crisp tortilla chips, cut day-old tortillas into wedges and shallow fry for 1–2 minutes or until crisp.

vegetables and noodles

Moroccan Potato and Pumpkin

(see photograph on page 84)

500g peeled and deseeded pumpkin

4 medium potatoes

400g can tomatoes in juice

1 cup vegetable stock

6 dried apricots

¼ teaspoon ground cinnamon

¼ teaspoon ground ginger

¼ teaspoon cayenne pepper

¼ cup lemon juice

1 tablespoon honey

1 Cut pumpkin into 4cm chunks. Peel potatoes and cut into eight large even-sized pieces.

2 Cook pumpkin and potatoes in tomatoes in juice and stock. Chop apricots. Add cinnamon, ginger, cayenne pepper, lemon juice and honey. Cover and simmer for 25–30 minutes. Serve on a platter.

Serves 6–8

Spinach and Pumpkin Curry

(see photograph opposite)

1kg pumpkin

1 large onion

2 cloves garlic

2 tablespoons oil

2 teaspoons Madras curry powder

½ teaspoon chilli powder

1½ cups water

3 bunches spinach

2 tomatoes

1 Peel pumpkin, deseed and cut into even-sized pieces. Peel onion and chop finely. Crush, peel and finely chop garlic.

2 Heat oil in a saucepan and sauté onion and garlic for 5 minutes. Add curry powder and chilli powder and cook for 1 minute or until spices smell fragrant. Add water and bring to the boil.

3 Add pumpkin and cook for 15 minutes or until pumpkin is just cooked. Wash spinach and remove stems. Tear coarse leaves into pieces. Add to pumpkin mixture and cook for 2–3 minutes. Cut tomatoes in half. Remove seeds and chop flesh into small cubes. Mix into pumpkin mixture. Serve on a platter.

Serves 6

Note: For this recipe a bunch of spinach is a mature spinach plant.

Pumpkin is easy to peel if partly cooked in the microwave. If you do this for this recipe, reduce the cooking time and reduce the cooking liquid by ½ cup.

Seedy Spiced Potatoes

6 medium potatoes

2 fresh red chillies

¼ cup peanut oil

1 teaspoon black mustard seeds

1 teaspoon ground coriander

½ teaspoon ground turmeric

½ teaspoon ground cumin

½ teaspoon salt

½ cup desiccated coconut

¼ cup lemon juice

1 tablespoon chopped fresh coriander
  or parsley

1 Peel potatoes and cut into wedges. Cook in boiling water for 10 minutes or until soft. Drain well. Deseed chillies and slice finely.

2 Heat oil in a frying pan and cook mustard seeds for 3–4 minutes or until they stop popping. Add coriander, turmeric, cumin and chillies to pan and cook for a few seconds until spices smell fragrant. Add potatoes, salt and coconut. Cook over a medium heat until potatoes start to colour.

3 Sprinkle lemon juice over potatoes and continue cooking until potatoes are crisp. Sprinkle coriander or parsley over and serve.

Serves 4–6

Note: These are superb served with a curry.

To cook potatoes quickly in the microwave, scrub them and wrap in cling wrap. Pierce each wrapped potato with a knife and microwave for 6–8 minutes on high power until cooked but firm and able to be sliced.

Potato Wedges with Spiked Mayo

6 large potatoes

3 tablespoons oil

2 teaspoons spicy Mexican wedge
 seasoning

SPIKED MAYO

½ cup mayonnaise

1 teaspoon lemon pepper seasoning

pinch cayenne pepper

1 Wash potatoes and cut into wedges. Pour oil into a roasting dish. Add potatoes and toss to coat. Sprinkle seasoning over.

2 Bake at 200°C for 30 minutes or until tender and golden, turning frequently during cooking. Serve hot with spiked mayo.

SPIKED MAYO

1 Mix mayonnaise, lemon pepper seasoning and cayenne pepper together.

Serves 6

Spiced Creamed Mushrooms

200g brown mushrooms

1 onion

1 tablespoon oil

¼ teaspoon ground cumin

¼ teaspoon garam masala

pinch cayenne pepper

1 teaspoon mustard powder

1 tablespoon tomato pureé

1 tablespoon lemon juice

1 cup low-fat cream

½ teaspoon salt

1 tablespoon chopped fresh parsley,
to garnish

1   Wipe mushrooms and trim. Slice if large. Peel onion and chop finely.

2   Heat oil in a saucepan and sauté onion for 2–3 minutes. Add cumin, garam masala and cayenne pepper and cook for 1 minute or until spices smell fragrant. Add mushrooms and cook for 1 minute. Mix mustard powder, tomato pureé, lemon juice and cream together. Add to mushroom mixture and cook until mixture is almost boiling.

3   Add salt and serve hot, garnished with chopped parsley.

Serves 3

Thai Noodles

1 onion

4 cloves garlic

2 tablespoons oil

2 tablespoons Thai red curry paste

1 tablespoon sugar

2 tablespoons Thai fish sauce (nam pla)

¼ cup chopped fresh coriander

1 teaspoon chilli powder

3 tablespoons lime juice

200g dried egg noodles

1 Peel onion and chop finely. Crush, peel and chop garlic.

2 Heat oil in a frying pan and sauté onion and garlic for 5 minutes or until lightly golden. Add curry paste and cook for 1 minute or until spices smell fragrant. Add sugar, fish sauce, coriander, chilli powder and lime juice. Stir to combine then remove from heat.

3 Cook noodles in boiling water to packet directions. Drain well and add to mixture in frying pan. Mix to coat noodles. Serve hot.

Serves 4

Note: Serve these with cooked chicken or fish.

Mexican Orange Salad

(see photograph opposite)

6 oranges, peeled and all white pith removed, sliced crosswise

2 red onions, sliced

90g toasted almonds, chopped

2 medium fresh red chillies, chopped

½ bunch fresh coriander

4 tablespoons fresh mint leaves

¼ bunch English spinach, leaves shredded

1 Place oranges, onions, almonds, chillies, coriander leaves and mint in a bowl, toss to combine and stand for 30 minutes.

2 Line a serving platter with spinach then pile salad on top.

Serves 6

Note: Garnish with extra red onion and serve with grilled meats or chicken.

Spicy Rice Tomato and Vegetables

(see photograph page 85)

1 tablespoon olive oil

1 onion, sliced

1 green pepper, diced

1 red chilli, seeded and finely chopped

¾ cup white rice

¾ cup quick-cooking brown rice

400g canned peeled tomatoes, undrained and roughly chopped

1½ cups vegetable stock or water

freshly ground black pepper

1 Heat oil in a large saucepan. Cook onion, pepper and chilli for 3–4 minutes.

2 Add rice, mix well and cook for 3–4 minutes. Add tomatoes to the pan with stock or water. Bring to the boil and simmer for 30 minutes or until liquid is absorbed and rice is tender. Season with pepper.

Serves 4

Spaghetti with Curried Chicken Sauce

500g spaghetti

1 red pepper

250g boneless, skinless chicken such
  as tenderloins

1 onion

1 clove garlic

1 teaspoon oil

2 teaspoons curry powder

1 cup natural unsweetened yoghurt

1 teaspoon salt

1 tablespoon chopped fresh coriander

1 Cook spaghetti in boiling, salted water according to packet directions.
   Drain well.

2 Cut pepper in half and grill until skin is blistered. When cool enough to
   handle, remove skin and cut pepper into thin strips. Set aside.

3 Remove any fat fro chicken and cut flesh into thin strips. Peel onion and chop
   finely. Crush, peel and chop garlic.

4 Heat oil in a saucepan. Sauté onion, garlic and chicken for 5 minutes or
   until onion is clear. Add curry powder and cook for 30 seconds to 1 minute
   or until curry smells fragrant. Add yoghurt and salt and bring to the boil and
   simmer for 2 minutes or until chicken is cooked.

5 Place spaghetti in serving bowls. Top with chicken sauce, red pepper strips
   and chopped coriander.

Serves 4

Squash with Green Onions

1 kg butternut squash, peeled and
  chopped

350g yellow or green patty pan squash

4 carrots, peeled and halved

2 teaspoons finely grated lime rind

1 tablespoon olive oil

freshly ground black pepper

150g feta cheese, crumbled

GREEN ONION DRESSING

12 spring onions, sliced

3 mild fresh green chillies, sliced

⅓ cup olive oil

¼ cup apple cider vinegar

2 tablespoons lime juice

1 Place butternut squash, patty pan squash, carrots, lime rind, 1 tablespoon
olive oil and black pepper to taste in a baking dish, toss to combine and
bake at 200°C for 30 minutes or until vegetables are golden and soft.

2 To make dressing, place spring onions, chillies, ⅓ cupolive oil, vinegar and
lime juice in a bowl and whisk to combine.

3 Place vegetables on a serving platter, scatter with feta cheese and drizzle
with dressing.

Serves 6

Malaysian Chicken with Noodles

1 onion

2 cloves garlic

oil spray

1 tablespoon prepared minced ginger

1 teaspoon prepared minced chilli

4 cups chicken stock

400g can chopped tomatoes in juice

300g cooked or uncooked skinless,
  boneless chicken

300g packet instant noodles

8 spinach leaves or

2 bok choy plants

1 tablespoon chopped fresh coriander

1 Peel onion and chop finely. Crush, peel and chop garlic. Spray a saucepan or clay pot with oil and saute onion, garlic, ginger and chilli for 5 minutes.

2 Add stock and tomatoes. Bring to the boil and add chicken and noodles. Cover and cook for 5 minutes, breaking up noodles to soften, or until chicken and noodles are cooked. Wash spinach or bok choy and add to pan. Cover and cook for 1–2 minutes. Sprinkle with coriander.

Serves 4

Stir-Fried Duck with Greens

1.2 kg Chinese barbecued or roasted duck

2 teaspoons vegetable oil

1 tablespoon Thai red curry paste

1 teaspoon shrimp paste

1 stalk fresh lemongrass, finely sliced, or ½ teaspoon dried lemongrass, soaked in hot water until soft

4 fresh red chillies

1 bunch Chinese broccoli or Swiss chard, chopped

1 tablespoon palm or brown sugar

2 tablespoons tamarind concentrate

1 tablespoon Thai fish sauce (nam pla)

1   Slice meat from duck, leaving the skin on, and cut into bite-sized pieces. Reserve as many of the cavity juices as possible.

2   Heat oil in a wok over a medium heat, add curry paste, shrimp paste, lemongrass and chillies and stir-fry for 3 minutes or until fragrant.

3   Add duck and reserved juices and stir-fry for 2 minutes or until coated in spice mixture and heated. Add broccoli or chard, sugar, tamarind and fish sauce and stir-fry for 3–4 minutes or until broccoli is wilted.

Serves 4

Minted Bean Curry

6 whole coriander plants, roots removed and washed, reserve leaves for another use

2 stalks fresh lemongrass, finely sliced, or 1 teaspoon dried lemongrass, soaked in hot water until soft

6 kaffir lime leaves, shredded

2 teaspoons palm or brown sugar

3 cups water

3 tablespoons Thai fish sauce (nam pla)

2 teaspoons peanut oil

3 small fresh green chillies, shredded

5cm piece fresh ginger, shredded

2 teaspoons Thai green curry paste

250g pea eggplant (aubergines)

250g snake (yard-long) or green beans, cut into 25mm pieces

440g canned tomatoes, drained and chopped

2 tablespoons tamarind concentrate

60g fresh mint leaves

1 Place coriander roots, lemongrass, lime leaves, sugar, water and fish sauce in a saucepan and bring to the boil. Reduce heat and simmer for 10 minutes. Strain, discard solids and set stock aside.

2 Heat oil in a wok or large saucepan over a medium heat, add chillies (if using), ginger and curry paste and stir-fry for 2–3 minutes or until fragrant. Add eggplant (aubergines) and beans and stir to coat with spice mixture. Stir in reserved stock and simmer for 10 minutes or until vegetables are tender. Add tomatoes and tamarind and simmer for 3 minutes or until hot. Stir in mint.

Serves 4

Note: Pea eggplant (aubergines) are tiny green eggplant (aubergines) about the size of green peas and are usually purchased still attached to the vine. They are used whole, eaten raw or cooked and have a bitter taste. If unavailable green peas can be used instead.

Stuffed Poblano Chillies

12 poblano chillies

Beef and Bean Filling

2 teaspoons vegetable oil

1 onion, chopped

320g beef mince

200g cooked or canned pinto beans, rinsed and drained

pinch cayenne pepper

½ cup tomato purée

TOMATILLO SAUCE

2 x 315g canned tomatillos, drained and finely chopped

1 onion, chopped

3 tablespoons chopped fresh coriander

½ cup vegetable stock

1 Place chillies in a hot frying pan or comal and cook until skins are blistered and charred. Place in a plastic food bag and stand for 10 minutes or until cool enough to handle. Carefully remove skins from chillies and cut a slit in the side of each one. Carefully remove seeds and membranes and set aside.

2 To make filling, heat oil in a frying pan over a medium heat, add onion and cook, stirring, for 2 minutes or until soft. Add beef and cook, stirring, for 3–4 minutes or until brown. Stir in beans, cayenne pepper and tomato purée, bring to simmering and simmer for 5 minutes or until mixture reduces and thickens. Spoon filling into chillies and place in a baking dish.

3 To make sauce, place tomatillos, onion, coriander and stock in a saucepan, bring to simmering and simmer for 5 minutes or until sauce reduces and thickens. Pour sauce over chillies and bake for 25 minutes or until chillies are heated through.

Makes 12

Noodles with Vegetable and Oyster Sauce

200g Chinese egg noodles

4 Chinese dried mushrooms

1 tablespoon oil

3 cloves garlic, chopped

1–2 red chillies, finely chopped

6 green onions, sliced

2 sticks celery, sliced

1 red pepper, sliced

2 cups shredded cabbage

3 tablespoons oyster sauce

1 tablespoon Thai fish sauce (nam pla)

1 tablespoon brown sugar

2 tablespoons water

¼ cup chopped peanuts

1   Cook egg noodles in a large saucepan of boiling water until tender, about 5 minutes. Drain well. Soak mushrooms in hot water for 20 minutes, then slice thinly.

2   Heat oil in a wok or large frying pan, add garlic and chillies and fry for 1 minutes.

3   Add all other ingredients except peanuts and noodles, bring to the boil. Lower heat and simmer for 2 minutes or until vegetables are tender but still crunchy.

4   Stir in cooked noodles and heat for 1 minute or until noodles are heated through. Serve sprinkled with peanuts.

Serves 6

Rice Noodles with Greens

350g thick fresh or dried rice noodles

1 tablespoon vegetable oil

2 tablespoons shredded fresh ginger

2 cloves garlic, crushed

250g Chinese broccoli (gai lan), chopped

125g asparagus, cut in half

3 tablespoons snipped fresh garlic chives

1/3 cup stock

2 tablespoons light soy sauce

1 teaspoon cornflour blended with 2 teaspoons water

1 Place noodles in a bowl and pour over boiling water to cover. If using fresh noodles, soak for 2 minutes; if using dried noodles, soak for 5-6 minutes or until soft. Drain well and set aside.

2 Heat oil in a wok or frying pan over a medium heat, add ginger and garlic and stir-fry for 1 minute. Add broccoli, asparagus , chives, stock and soy sauce and stir-fry for 2 minutes.

3 Add noodles to wok and stir-fry for 4 minutes or until heated through. Stir in cornflour mixture and cook for 1 minute or until mixture thickens.

Serves 4

side dishes

Spicy Potato Roti

(see photograph on page 102)

½ cup unsweetened natural yoghurt

1 teaspoon prepared minced ginger

½ –1 teaspoon chilli powder

3 tablespoons chopped fresh coriander

1½ cups boiling water

1½ cups instant mashed potatoes

¼ cup rice flour

1 teaspoon sesame oil

1 Mix yoghurt, ginger, chilli powder, coriander and boiling water together. Mix potato in until smooth. Add rice flour and mix to combine.

2 Heat a heavy-based ovenproof frying pan until very hot. Grease base with sesame oil.

3 Spread potato mixture into pan and bake at 200°C for 20–25 minutes or until lightly golden. Serve with your selection of chicken, meat or fish.

Serves 6

Note: If you like hot fare, use a teaspoon of chilli powder. For a lower heat use half a teaspoon.

Spicy Naan Bread

(see photograph opposite)

4 naan bread

50g butter

1 teaspoon mild curry powder

2 tablespoons sesame seeds

1 Cut each naan bread into four pieces. Melt butter in a frying pan and add curry powder and sesame seeds. Cook for 1 minute. Brush mixture over the top of the bread pieces. Grill until lightly golden. Turn and grill until golden on other side. Serve warm.

Makes 16

Note: This is so delicious it can be enjoyed on its own, perhaps with a tasty relish as a delicious snack.

Naan bread can be bought fresh or frozen from the supermarket.

Spicy Sprinkle for Vegetables or Salads

½ cup peanuts

1 tablespoon toasted sesame seeds

¼ teaspoon ground cumin

½ teaspoon ground coriander

½ teaspoon fenugreek seeds

½ teaspoon salt

½ teaspoon cracked black pepper

½ teaspoon thyme

1 Roughly chop peanuts. Mix peanuts, sesame seeds, cumin, coriander, fenugreek, salt and pepper together in a small ovenproof dish.

2 Bake at 180°C for 10–15 minutes or until peanuts are golden. Remove from oven and mix thyme through. Store in an airtight container and use to sprinkle over cooked vegetables or salads.

Makes about ½ cup

Note: To toast sesame and fenugreek seeds, place in a frying pan and cook over a medium heat until lightly golden.

Lime Chutney

6 limes

2 tablespoons salt

1 onion

1 cup seedless raisins

2 tablespoons grated root ginger

1 tablespoon yellow mustard seeds

1 cup white vinegar

2 cups brown sugar

3 dried chillies

1 Cut limes into eighths and place in a nonmetallic bowl. Sprinkle with salt, mixing to coat. Cover and leave at room temperature for 24 hours. Stir occasionally.

2 Peel and coarsely chop onion. Place limes and juice that has come from them, onion, raisins and ginger in a food processor and process until coarsely chopped. Place mixture in a heavy-based, non-aluminium saucepan with mustard seeds, vinegar, sugar and chillies. Bring to the boil then reduce heat and simmer, uncovered, for 1–1½ hours or until thick. Stir occasionally to prevent catching.

3 Spoon into hot, clean, dry jars and seal while hot. Serve with a meat curry.

Makes 2 cups

Note: There is no really quick way to make this relish but it is easy and very delicious. Salting the limes helps reduce the bitter flavour often present in lime chutney.

Indian Pancakes

(see photograph opposite)

3 green onions

1½ cups rice flour

1 teaspoon salt

½ teaspoon baking powder

400ml can coconut milk

oil

1. Trim and finely chop green onions. Mix rice flour, salt, baking powder and green onions together. Add half the coconut milk and whisk until smooth. Whisk in remaining coconut milk.

2. Grease a small frying pan with oil. Spoon about 2 tablespoons of batter into pan. Cook over a medium heat until lightly brown. Turn and cook the other side. Keep warm and serve with curries.

Makes 25

Fresh Mint Chutney

(see photograph opposite)

4 green onions

2 fresh green chillies

1 cup firmly packed fresh mint leaves

¼ teaspoon salt

1 teaspoon sugar

1 teaspoon garam masala

¼ cup lime juice

1. Trim green onions and chop roughly. Deseed chillies and chop roughly.

2. Place green onions, chillies, mint leaves, salt, sugar, garam masala and lime juice in a food processor or blender. Process until smooth.

3. Serve as an accompaniment to curries or roast lamb.

Makes ½ cup

Note: For a different flavour, add 2–3 tablespoons of yoghurt to this.

index